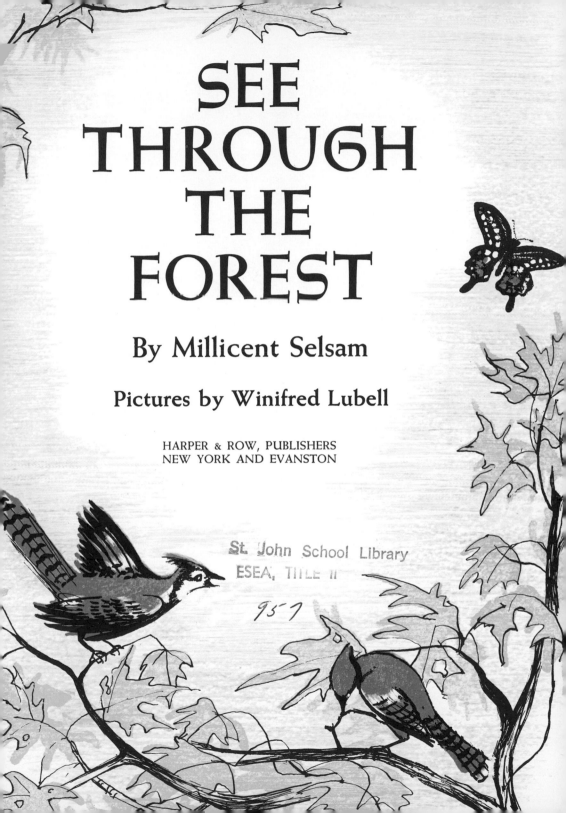

SEE THROUGH THE FOREST

By Millicent Selsam

Pictures by Winifred Lubell

HARPER & ROW, PUBLISHERS
NEW YORK AND EVANSTON

SEE THROUGH THE FOREST

WE are in a forest.

In the meadows outside, the sun beats down hot and strong. The wind bends the grass. The air is dry. But here in the forest, everything is different.

The branches of the trees sway softly in a faint breeze. The shade is deep, except where splashes of sunlight touch the tree trunks and the forest floor. The air is cool and still. It is damp too. The moisture that rises from the soil and plants in the forest stays locked inside it. The forest has its own climate.

But the forest climate is not the same from bottom to top. On the shady ground, it is moist and cool. In the breezy treetops, it is warm, dry, and light. In between it changes gradually.

The forest is like a tall building. The trees rise like posts holding up a roof of leaves. Inside this forest building are many plant and animal tenants living on different floors. Each floor has its own special climate—light or dark, damp or dry, warm or cool. And each floor has its own special tenants.

This is the basement of the forest. At the top, there is a layer of dead and dying leaves. Here a host of small animals dig and scurry around in a dark wet world.

You can easily pick out the beetles and ants. But find the millipedes, called "thousand-legged worms" even though they are not worms and have nowhere near a thousand legs. The centipedes look like them but have fewer legs. Tiny spider-like mites are all over the place. But the springtails almost crowd out the other tenants. Their tails seem to spring into the air when they hop from one place to another.

Thin white threads of molds weave in and out everywhere. There are millions and millions of bacteria here
too, but you can't see them because they are so tiny.
The molds and bacteria feed on the dead leaves. As they
do, they break down the food in the dead leaves into
minerals that enrich the soil.

Here and there tiny plants are beginning to push out
of their seed coats. In the cool dark damp of the forest
soil, the seeds of forest trees get their start.

Under the leafy layer, there is a rich spongy soil in which there are not so many animals. Here, between the roots of trees and other plants, are tunnels dug by earthworms, moles, chipmunks, and woodchucks.

The tiny tunnels are those of earthworms. They swallow the soil and pass it through their long bodies as they wriggle through the ground. That little animal with a wedge-shaped head and strong front claws is a mole. It is scooping out a new side tunnel and looking for earthworms to eat. The ever-hungry shrew is chasing a mouse in an underground passage made by a chipmunk. The woodchuck is taking a nap in his burrow.

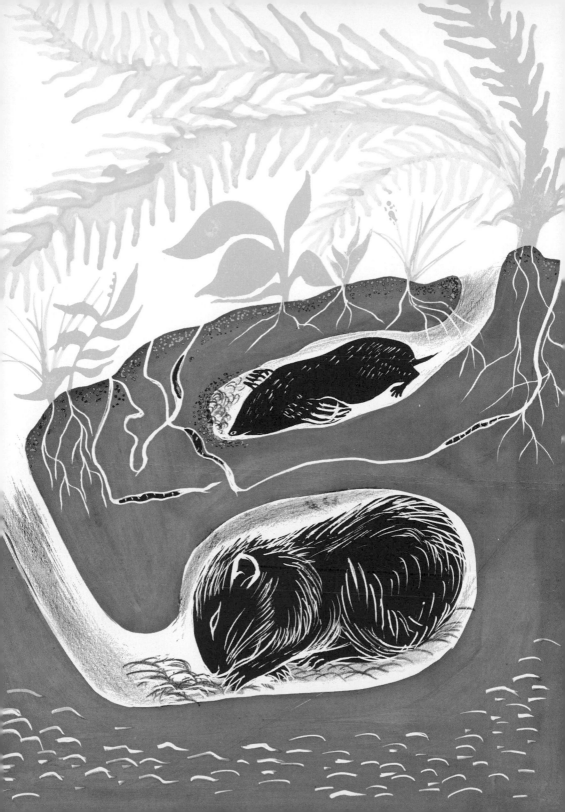

In the winter, the lower basement of the forest gets many new tenants from higher up. Ants and beetles, spiders, toads, and salamanders creep down into snug holes. Earthworms squirm down deeper. Chipmunks and woodchucks lengthen their burrows, go to the lowest parts, and sleep there through the long cold winter. Even animals from outside the forest come here to find protection in the forest soil. The soil is warmer in the forest because it is covered by a blanket of fallen leaves.

Just above the basement is the ground floor of the forest. In the spring, before all the light is shut out by the roof of green leaves, the forest floor is gay with wild flowers.

Violets bloom at the foot of that giant oak tree. Spring beauty covers the ground with a delicate mist. The flowers that look like white pantaloons hanging upside down are called Dutchman's-breeches. The jack-in-the-pulpit has a striped hood (the pulpit) and a light green stalk (the jack) that bears the tiny flowers. The ferns are still coiled up in fiddleheads that will unfurl soon.

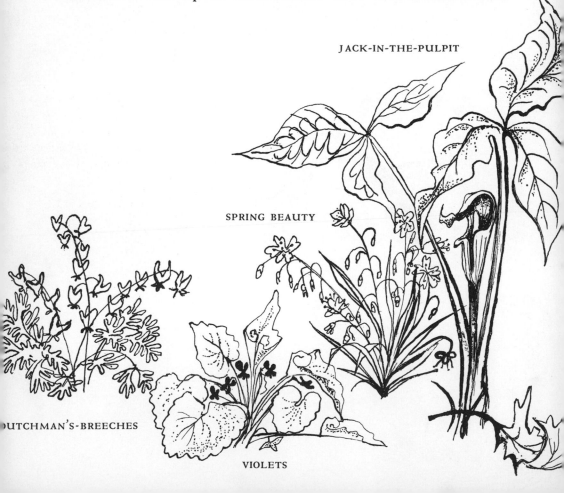

JACK-IN-THE-PULPIT

SPRING BEAUTY

DUTCHMAN'S-BREECHES

VIOLETS

OLEHEADS

In summer, when the trees are in full leaf, the green roof of the forest closes over. Now most of the forest floor is covered with the outspread fronds of ferns, the stems of grasses, and the leaves of many plants that bloomed earlier.

But here and there some plants are blossoming in the shade. The feathery-looking bedstraw has tiny white flowers. The flowers of the touch-me-not glow in the dim light. The fruits of this plant spring open at a touch and give the plant its name.

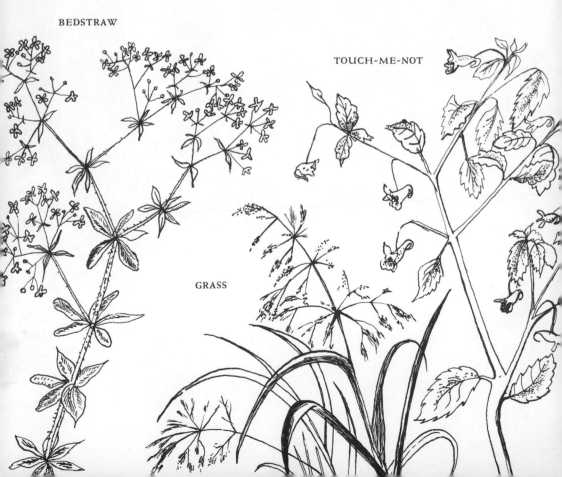

BEDSTRAW

TOUCH-ME-NOT

GRASS

Where are the animals of the forest? They seem to be hiding. But if you sit down on a log and stay quite still, you will see them.

There below that mushroom is a salamander. Gliding on a wet trail near it is a woodland snail, crunching leaves as it goes. The box turtle was eating mushrooms, but something must have scared him. He has pulled in his legs and head and is lying closed up in his boxlike shell.

In that great big rotting log on the ground, thousands of termites are swallowing the partly decayed wood. The dainty ovenbird is walking over to the log on its flat little feet. Look behind the ovenbird, and see its round nest covered on top and open in front like an old-fashioned outdoor oven. Inside are four speckled eggs.

Another ground-floor bird is over by the giant oak tree. It is the woodcock, who never sees what it eats. It pokes its long bill into the soft forest floor and feels for earthworms.

What is that soft shadow behind the oak tree? Here at last is one of the larger forest animals. It is a white-tailed deer browsing on the small plants of the forest floor.

Imagine yourself in the forest after the sun sets. Night is falling. The shadows grow darker. They are broken only by patches of silvery moonlight. Listen to the soft rustling. Now you can see the ground-floor animals who hide by day and hunt for their food only at night.

In the deep shadows, a family of striped skunks is taking a walk. Don't disturb them! You would have to leave your comfortable seat on the log if the skunks suddenly turned around, raised their tails, and sprayed their special skunk smell anywhere near you.

This is family night in the forest. A mother raccoon and her five little babies have just come out of their hollow tree trunk. They're going to hunt for their dinner.

Because you sat so still, a red fox has come close. He is sniffing at the ground where a little white-footed mouse has just dived into a hole. If the fox doesn't reach this mouse, his keen eyes and sharp ears will be sure to find another little mouse to eat.

The fox eats the mouse, who eats the seeds and nuts of the forest. Without the forest trees and plants, there would be no food for the fox!

Now get up from your seat on the forest floor. You can lean against the giant oak and keep your eyes on the next floor of the forest, the level where the shrubs grow. Over there is a witch hazel bush. The bark and leaves of this bush give us the witch hazel we keep in bottles in our medicine cabinets. Other bushes grow here too in the little light that reaches them through the leafy roof of the forest.

A black racer snake is resting on the branches of the witch hazel. When he does move, he goes fast. He seizes any frog, bird, or small animal he can find in his path and swallows it.

Everywhere among the twigs of the shrubs gleam the silver wheels of the orb-weaver spiders. The spiders are hiding in rolled up leaves near the webs. There they wait for any insect that may get tangled in the sticky threads of their webs. And there are good pickings!

Thousands of insects are getting their food from the low growth of the forest. Caterpillars of all kinds are munching on leaves. There are beetles and bumblebees and butterflies and green katydids. You can hardly turn over a leaf without finding some insect. Especially plant lice. Millions of them are sucking the juices from the leaves and bark of the shrubs.

The enormous number of forest insects are feeding either on plants or on other insects. They in turn are food for many a bird!

Lots of birds are searching this level of the forest for their insect dinners. Look at the lower trunks of the three hickory trees in the center. A whole little company of black-capped chickadees, a nuthatch, and a downy woodpecker are swarming over the rough bark. Both the chickadees and the nuthatch have black caps, but only the chickadees have black throats. The nuthatch seems to be upside down! But there's nothing wrong. Nuthatches usually go down a tree head first. The chickadees and the nuthatch are feeding on the insects they find in the bark of the trees. So is the downy woodpecker. Watch him as his strong bill drills into the bark. Then his long tongue, with barbs like fishhooks at the end, shoots into the hole and comes out with a squirming grub sticking to the end.

That flash of blue in the bushes is a brilliant indigo bunting. Near by a little black and white striped warbler is hunting for caterpillars.

DOGWOOD

Now let's climb up into the next story of the forest building. We can make it easily up the maple tree, hook a leg over this big branch, and sit in a sea of leaves. How different it is here from the bottom of the forest—so much lighter and brighter and drier! From our snug seat we can see the tops of dogwood and sassafras trees. It's nice to rest here and wonder why there are three kinds of leaves on a sassafras tree, and why the twigs of the dogwood tree branch like a road with a left and right fork.

What a noise we made as we climbed! It scared the tenants of the forest trees away.

SASSAFRAS

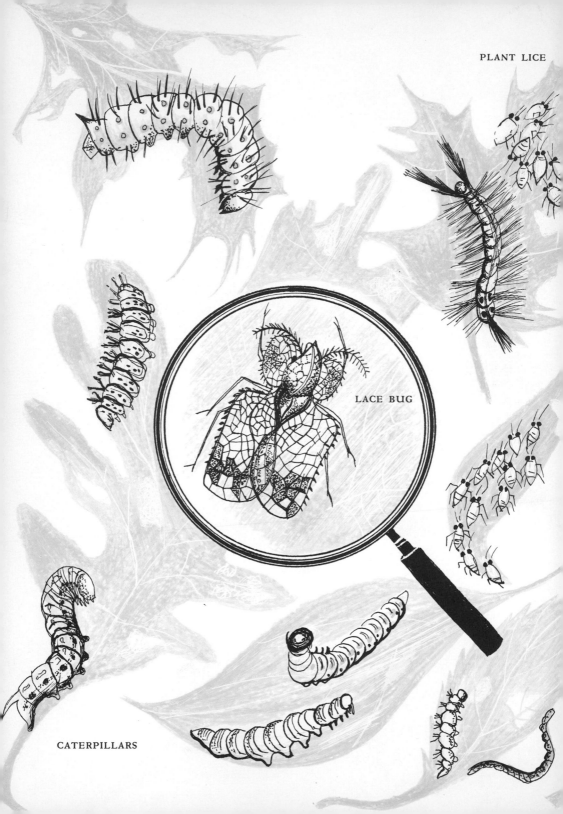

PLANT LICE

LACE BUG

CATERPILLARS

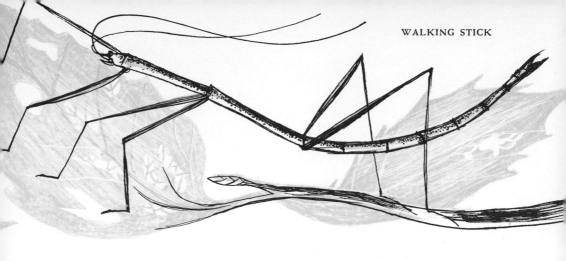

But even while we climbed, the plant lice kept sucking away at the hundreds of thousands of leaves we can see from our perch. The caterpillars kept eating. The tree hoppers and lace bugs kept making tiny holes in the leaves to suck their juices. And the walking sticks kept taking bites out of tender leaves.

The birds left this lively party of insects when we climbed our tree. Now they are gathering again. They are quite different from the ones we saw below.

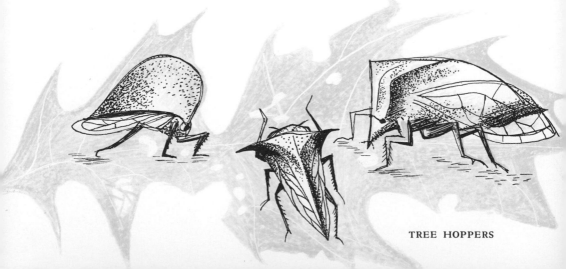

TREE HOPPERS

The scarlet tanager makes a bright splash of color in this sea of green. He is eating one caterpillar after another. Look at your watch and time him. In one minute he gulps down thirty-five caterpillars! If he did this for only one hour each day, he would eat 2100 caterpillars in one day, and about 15,000 in a week. This bird certainly helps to keep down the number of insects in the forest!

There goes a little red-eyed vireo. He is called a "preacher" bird, because he keeps on singing all through the day. Watch him as his head turns from side to side. Suddenly he stops singing and snatches a ladybird beetle from the underside of a leaf. The vireo eats the ladybird beetle that eats the plant lice that suck the plant juices from the leaves. Without the green leaves of the forest, there would be no food for the birds.

Noisy screams make us turn to look at two bluejays. They are eating the fruits of the wild apple tree. The pulpy part of the fruit is digested, but the seeds will go right through the birds' digestive tracts and come out in their droppings. Since the bluejays are always flying around, the seeds may fall some distance away. This is how bluejays and other birds of the forest help to spread the seeds of forest trees to new places. Without them, the seeds would fall to the ground beneath the parent tree, where they would have little chance to grow.

Birds and insects are not the only ones who get up to this level of the forest.

Graceful gray squirrels leap from branch to branch to nibble at acorns and hickory nuts. They often run up and down through the invisible floors of the forest. But their real home in the forest is up here. Watch that big fellow balance himself with his bushy tail as he leaps!

If we could stay on our perch until dusk, we would see more. A flying squirrel swoops down in the gloom. It doesn't really fly, but spreads open two furry flaps of skin that go from foreleg to hind leg, and glides through the air. In one leap, it can go about the distance of a short city block.

A gray scraggly looking opossum is in the next tree. It has its tail curled around one branch, while its grasping feet are clinging to another branch.

A tiny little movement makes us notice a small tree frog. If we could grab it, we could feel the sticky pads on the tips of its fingers and toes. These help it to stick to any surface—leaves, branches, or tree trunks.

With their special tails and feet, the gray squirrel, the flying squirrel, the opossum, and the tree frog are well suited to their life up here in the branches.

Now we are going to the very top of the forest. To do that we have to climb to the top of that tall oak. We have no sticky pads on our toes, no tails to curl around a branch, no bushy tails for balance, no furry skin gliders. It's hard for us to get up so high, holding on with just hands and feet. But we climb and climb through the floors of the forest building until at last we stick our heads through the leafy roof.

It's like breaking through the surface of the water. Suddenly there is hot sunshine and wind. The ground floor of the forest with its dim light and cool air seems far away.

Above us a great big bird wheels in the sky. By the way the light flashes on its red tail, we know it is a red-tailed hawk. Can the hawk see anything from way up there? Suddenly he goes zooming down. We hold our breath as he dives past. In a few seconds he rises again, and we know that the hawk has the keenest of eyes. In his sharp curved talons is a gray squirrel.

A tiny blue warbler darts out from the top branches, catching the insects that fly in the sunshine above the forest. This warbler lives in the highest branches of the trees, just as some people live on the top floors of an apartment building. He has relatives down on the lower floors—the black and white warbler, who keeps to the lower trunks and branches, and the ovenbird, who patrols the ground.

How different the tenants of the treetops are from the ones that live on the floor of the forest! The springtails and centipedes of the dark, wet forest basement could not live in the dry, airy climate of the forest roof. The flying squirrel of the upper forest floors could not burrow in the ground like a mole.

Some of the forest animals go up and down through the different forest levels. But they do tend to spend most of their time on the particular level where the conditions suit them best.

Even though there are different layers of life in the forest, they are not really separate from each other. Each part of the forest is closely linked to every other part. It is a community of plants and animals that live together, and act on each other. There is not one single animal or plant in the forest that isn't affected by the others around it.

When a woodpecker drills his holes in a tree, he is affecting the lives of the whole forest community. Take away the woodpeckers of the forest, and the wood-boring beetles they eat would multiply. They would go right along making holes in the bark and weakening the flow of sap to the trees until most of the trees died.

When the scarlet tanager and other insect-feeding birds eat thousands of caterpillars apiece each week, they too are affecting the lives of all the other forest creatures. If the numbers of such birds should suddenly decrease, there would be such crowds of insects chewing up the leaves that the trees and other plants of the forest would not last long.

When the ladybird beetle eats the plant lice that suck the leaves, it too is helping to keep the whole forest community alive. Without the ladybird beetles, the millions of plant lice would destroy the very plants they eat.

Every living thing in the forest is linked to the others around it. What happens to one member of the forest community may touch the lives of all the other plants and animals in it.

DATE DUE
